THE NATURE KIDS GUIDE TO
JAGUARS

DAVID ANDERSON

LP Media Inc. Publishing
Text copyright © 2026 by LP Media Inc.
All rights reserved.

For information address LP Media Inc. Publishing,
30012 Variolite St NW, Princeton MN 55371
www.lpmedia.org

Publication Data

Jaguars
The Nature Kid's Guide to Jaguars — First edition.

Summary: "Learn all about Jaguars, the Nature Kid Way"
— Provided by publisher.

ISBN: 979-8-89818-120-8

[1. Jaguars – Non-Fiction] I. Title.

Title: The Nature Kid's Guide to Jaguars

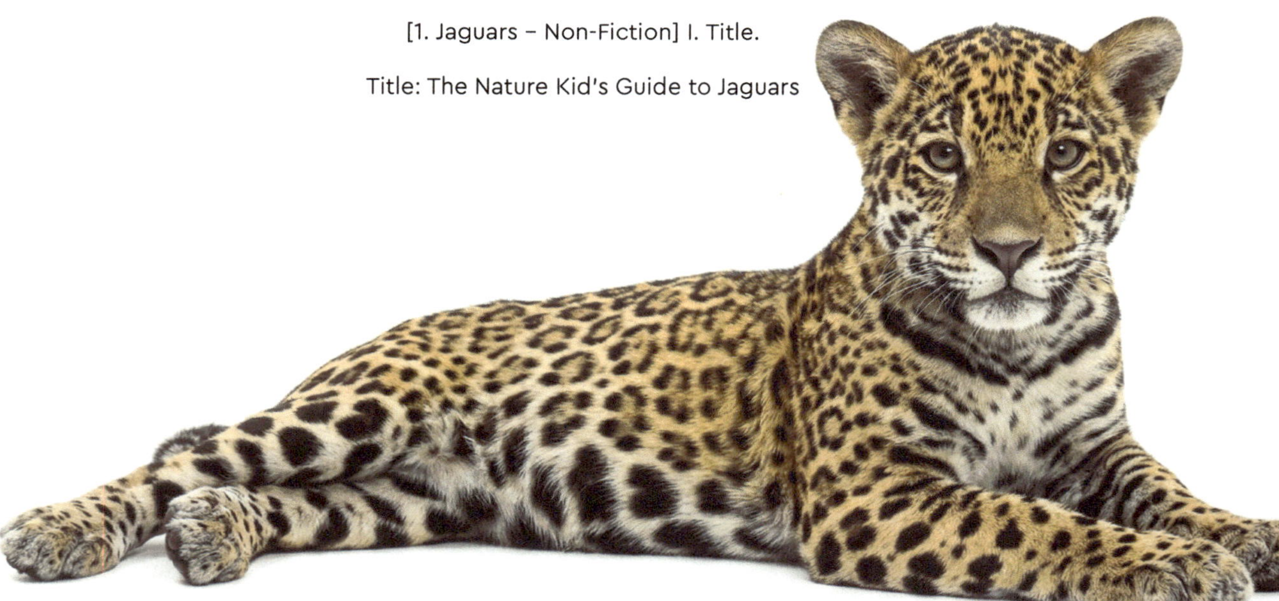

CONTENTS

JUNGLE HOME

Most jaguars live in Central and South America. The Amazon rainforest is home to many. They are the largest wild cats in the Americas.

Growl! A jaguar rests on a thick branch. Its spotted coat hides in shadows.

Jaguars need hot, wet places to live. Rainforests are perfect for them. Tall trees grow close together there. Vines hang from branches. The forest floor stays dark and damp.

These big cats love fresh water. They live near rivers and swamps. Some live in grasslands too. But water must be close by.

Thick plants help jaguars hide and hunt. They rest in shady spots when the sun is high. Jaguars feel at home where trees meet water. This warm, wet world gives them everything they need.

WILD WANDERERS

A male jaguar's home range can be over 300 square miles. That is truly huge!

Rustle! A jaguar moves through tall grass. It searches for prey.

Jaguars live in 19 countries! They roam from Mexico all the way to Argentina. But most jaguars live in Brazil. About half of all jaguars in the world live there!

All jaguars are the same species. But they can look different. The biggest jaguars live in Brazil's wetlands. They can weigh over 300 pounds! Jaguars in Mexico are smaller.

Most jaguars have golden fur with black spots. But some jaguars are all black! People call them black panthers. Only a few jaguars still visit the United States. They cross the border from Mexico into Arizona.

BIG CATS

Stretch! A jaguar stretches its big, strong body in the jungle.

Jaguars are the largest cats in the Americas. They are also the third largest cats in the world. Only tigers and lions are bigger.

Male jaguars weigh more than females. A big male can weigh up to 350 pounds. Females usually weigh around 170 pounds.

Jaguars have short, thick legs and bodies built for power. They are smaller than tigers but much stronger for their size.

A jaguar's head is wider than a leopard's head. This gives it a stronger bite.

SPOTTED STYLE

Snarl! A jaguar shows its golden fur, covered in dark spots.

Jaguars have beautiful spotted coats. Their fur is golden or tan with black markings called **rosettes**. Each rosette has a ring shape with spots inside.

No two jaguars look the same. Each cat has its own pattern. It is like a fingerprint!

Some jaguars look all black. They still have spots, but the fur is so dark you can barely see them. These dark cats are called black panthers.

A jaguar's spots help it blend in with sunlight and shadows on the forest floor.

SUPER SENSES

Snap! A jaguar turns its ears. It hears a sound far away.

Jaguars have amazing senses. Their eyes see well in the dark. This helps them hunt at night.

Their ears can turn in different directions. They pick up tiny sounds from far away. A jaguar can hear a rustle of leaves or small movements in the thick forest

Jaguars also have a strong sense of smell. They use their nose to find other jaguars and track down prey.

Jaguars can see six times better than humans in low light.

HIDDEN HUNTER

14

Shhh! A jaguar lays on the forest floor. It's spots help it blend in.

Jaguars are great at hiding. Their spotted coats help them blend in. Light and shadow mix on the forest floor. The spots break up the jaguar's shape.

This hiding is called **camouflage**. It helps jaguars sneak up on prey. They can get close without being seen.

Jaguars stay very still when they hide. They can wait for hours. They do not move at all.

Jaguars often hunt from trees. They wait for an animal to walk below then ponce on top!

15

MEATY MEALS

A jaguar waits by the river. It is trying to catch a fish!

Jaguars are **carnivores**, which means they eat meat. They hunt many kinds of animals.

Jaguars catch deer, wild pigs, and capybaras. They also eat fish, turtles, and even small alligators! They can catch over 85 different kinds of animals!

Jaguars kill their prey quickly. They have the strongest bite of all big cats. They often drag their meal to a safe place to eat alone.

A Jaguars bite is so strong it can crush a turtle shell.

SNEAK ATTACK

Pounce! A jaguar leaps from behind a tree and lands on its prey.

Jaguars are sneaky hunters. They do not chase their prey for long distances. Instead, they creep close before attacking.

A jaguar moves slowly through the jungle. It stays low to the ground, and its soft paws make almost no sound on the forest floor.

When the jaguar gets close enough, it pounces! It jumps on the animal from behind or from the side. The attack happens very fast.

Jaguars often hunt near water, too. They wait by rivers where animals come to drink.

TOP CAT

A jaguar stands tall on a fallen log. It is king here.

Jaguars are **apex predators**. This means no other animal hunts them. They are at the top of the food chain.

Being at the top matters. Apex predators help keep nature in balance. Jaguars hunt other animals. This controls how many animals live in one area.

Without jaguars, there would be too many deer. The deer would eat too many plants. Then the forest would get sick.

Jaguars kill prey with one powerful bite to the head.

STAY SAFE

Hiss! A jaguar crouches low, its eyes scanning for danger.

Adult jaguars have no predators. But jaguar cubs face more dangers. Eagles and large snakes sometimes hunt young cubs.

Mother jaguars work hard to keep their babies safe. They hide their cubs in dens under thick plants or between rocks. The spotted fur on cubs helps them blend in and stay hidden.

Adult jaguars climb trees to rest safely. They also swim across rivers to escape forest fires.

Jaguar cubs stay with their mother for about two years before living alone.

SWIM STRONG

24

Splash! A jaguar dives into a river and swims fast.

Jaguars are excellent swimmers. They love the water and swim often.

These big cats have strong legs. Their powerful muscles push them through rivers and streams with ease.

Jaguars swim to cross rivers. They also catch fish and turtles in the water. During the rainy season, some jaguars even swim across flooded forests.

Jaguars can swim over a mile without rest. They are one of the few big cats that love water.

NIGHT PROWL

Thump! A jaguar walks through the dark jungle. Its eyes glow.

Jaguars are most active at dawn and dusk. This means jaguars like the in-between hours when it is not too bright and not too dark. Some jaguars also hunt at night when it is fully dark.

Their eyes work well in low light. Special cells inside their eyes reflect light, which helps them see in the dark.

Jaguars rest during the hottest parts of the day. They save energy for cooler hours.

A jaguar's eyes have a mirror-like layer that helps them see and makes their eyes glow at night.

LONE RANGER

FUN FACT!
Jaguars use scent marking and roaring to communicate without meeting face to face.

A jaguar walks alone through the dark forest.

Jaguars live alone. They do not form groups like lions or wolves. These big cats like to be by themselves.

Each jaguar has its own **territory**. A territory is an area where one animal lives and hunts. A male jaguar's territory can be as big as 50 square miles! That is bigger than some towns.

Jaguars let other jaguars know to stay away. They scratch trees to leave claw marks. They also leave their scent on trees and rocks. These smells and marks are like "keep out" signs. Other jaguars know this area is already taken.

CALLING MATES

Howl! A jaguar calls out in the night. The sound echoes through the jungle.

Jaguars make loud sounds to find each other. Males roar to let females know where they are. These calls travel far through the jungle.

Female jaguars also call out. They make sounds when they are ready to meet a male.

Jaguars also use smell to find mates. Their scent marks attract other jaguars during mating seaon.

Female jaguars call for mates about six days at a time. Calls travel up to two miles!

CUDDLY CUBS

Squeak! A tiny black jaguar cub waits for it's mother to return.

Jaguar cubs are born with their eyes closed. They cannot see for about two weeks. The cubs are very small and helpless at first.

Newborn cubs have soft, fuzzy fur with spots already visible on their coats. These tiny cubs drink milk from their mother for several months.

Cubs grow quickly on this diet. They start eating meat when they are a few months old. Young jaguars stay with their mother for about two years before living on their own.

A mother jaguar usually gives birth to one to four cubs at a time. Most litters have two cubs.

MOM KNOWS

Wow! A mother jaguar carries her cub gently in her mouth.

Mother jaguars take care of their cubs alone. The father does not help, so mom does all the work.

She teaches her cubs important skills. They watch her hunt and learn by copying what she does.

Mother jaguars keep their cubs safe in hidden dens. They move them to new spots if danger comes near. Cubs also practice climbing and swimming with mom watching close by.

A mother jaguar's cubs weigh about 2 pounds when they are born.

FALLING FORESTS

Crack! A tree falls in the jungle. A jaguar watches.

Jaguars are losing their homes. People cut down forests to make farms and roads. This destroys the places where jaguars live.

When forests disappear, jaguars have less space to roam. They cannot find enough food or safe places to rest.

Some jaguars wander into towns looking for food. This is dangerous for both jaguars and people.

Jaguars have lost about half of the land they once lived on. Scientists create safe paths between forests so jaguars can travel safely.

SAVING JAGUARS

Stomp! A jaguar walks through a protected forest. It is safe here.

People work to save jaguars. They make safe places called reserves. Jaguars can live there without danger.

Scientists study jaguars. They use special cameras. The cameras take pictures when animals walk by. This helps people learn where jaguars live.

Some groups plant new trees. The trees connect jaguar homes. These green paths let jaguars travel safely.

Camera traps have photographed over 2,000 jaguars. Each one has a unique spot pattern.

GLOSSARY

rosettes
Ring-shaped spots with smaller spots inside them on a jaguar's fur.

camouflage
Colors or patterns that help an animal hide by blending in with the area around it.

carnivores
Animals that eat only meat.

apex predators
Animals at the top that no other animals hunt.

territory
An area where one animal lives and hunts.